HAL•LEONARD INSTRUMENTAL PLAY-ALONG

TENOR SAX

2ND EDITION

Taylor Swift

To access audio visit:
www.halleonard.com/mylibrary

Enter Code
2639-8287-1999-6670

Audio Arrangements by Peter Deneff

ISBN 978-1-61780-574-5

HAL•LEONARD® CORPORATION

7777 W. BLUEMOUND RD. P.O. BOX 13819 MILWAUKEE, WI 53213

Visit Hal Leonard Online at
www.halleonard.com

BACK TO DECEMBER

Words and Music by
TAYLOR SWIFT

TENOR SAX

BLANK SPACE

TENOR SAX

Words and Music by TAYLOR SWIFT,
MAX MARTIN and SHELLBACK

FIFTEEN

TENOR SAX

Words and Music by
TAYLOR SWIFT

I KNEW YOU WERE TROUBLE

TENOR SAX

Words and Music by TAYLOR SWIFT,
SHELLBACK and MAX MARTIN

LOVE STORY

TENOR SAX

Words and Music by
TAYLOR SWIFT

MEAN

TENOR SAX

Words and Music by
TAYLOR SWIFT

OUR SONG

TENOR SAX

Words and Music by
TAYLOR SWIFT

15

PICTURE TO BURN

TENOR SAX

Words and Music by TAYLOR SWIFT
and LIZ ROSE

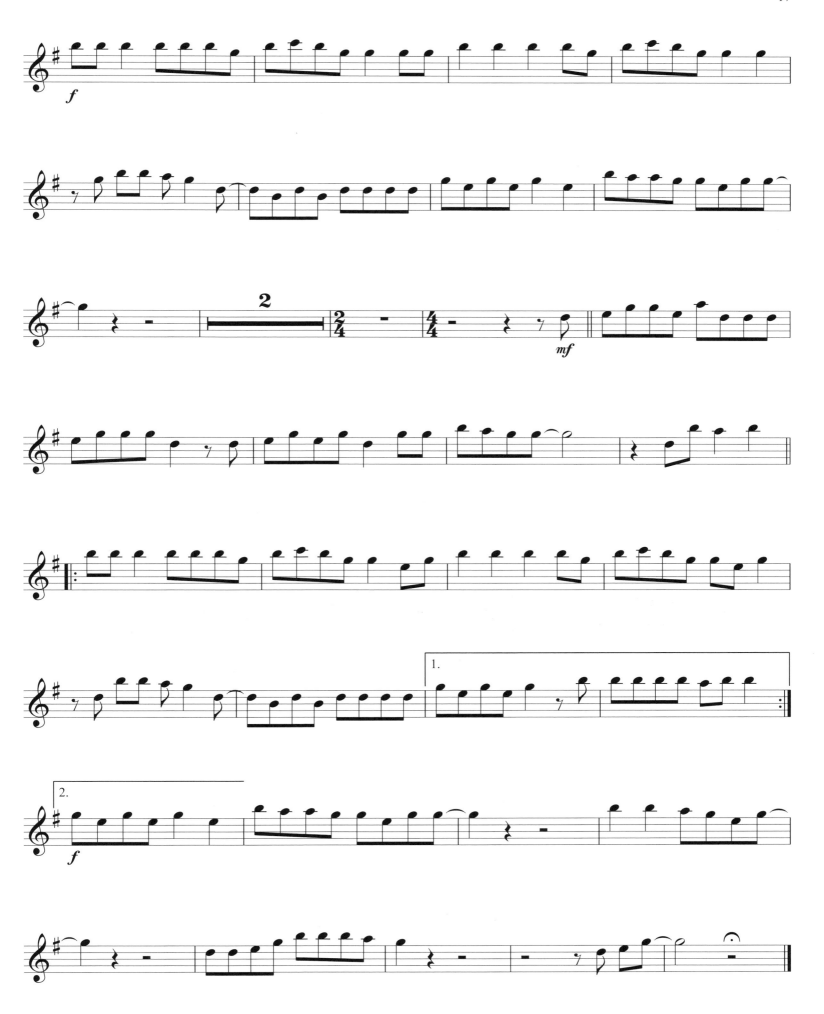

SHAKE IT OFF

TENOR SAX

Words and Music by TAYLOR SWIFT,
MAX MARTIN and SHELLBACK

SHOULD'VE SAID NO

TENOR SAX

Words and Music by
TAYLOR SWIFT

TEARDROPS ON MY GUITAR

TENOR SAX

Words and Music by TAYLOR SWIFT
and LIZ ROSE

22

TENOR SAX

Words and Music by TAYLOR SWIFT,
SHELLBACK and MAX MARTIN

WE ARE NEVER EVER GETTING BACK TOGETHER

TENOR SAX

Words and Music by TAYLOR SWIFT,
SHELLBACK and MAX MARTIN

WHITE HORSE

TENOR SAX

Words and Music by TAYLOR SWIFT
and LIZ ROSE

YOU BELONG WITH ME

TENOR SAX

Words and Music by TAYLOR SWIFT
and LIZ ROSE